How I Clean My Room

by Robin Nelson

first step nonfiction

Lerner Publications Company · Minneapolis

LERNER

SOURCE™

Expand learning beyond the printed book. Download free, complementary educational resources for this book from our website, www.lerneresource.com.

The images in this book are used with the permission of: © Todd Strand/Independent Picture Service.

Front Cover: © Laura Westlund/Independent Picture Service.

Main body text set in ITC Avant Garde Gothic Std Medium 21/25.
Typeface provided by Adobe Systems.

Lerner Publications Company
A division of Lerner Publishing Group, Inc.
241 First Avenue North
Minneapolis, MN 55401 USA

For reading levels and more information, look up this title at www.lernerbooks.com.

Library of Congress Cataloging-in-Publication Data

Nelson, Robin, 1971–
    How I clean my room / by Robin Nelson.
        pages   cm. — (First step nonfiction—responsibility in action)
    Includes index.
    ISBN 978–1–4677–3634–3 (lib. bdg. : alk. paper)
    ISBN 978–1–4677–3649–7 (eBook)
    1. House cleaning—Juvenile literature. I. Title.
TX324.N456 2014
648'5—dc23   2013028495

Manufactured in the United States of America
1 – BP – 12/31/13

Table of Contents

Cleanup Time!

My room is a mess!

I need to clean up.

Cleaning Up Clothes

First, I pick up my clothes.

I put dirty clothes in the **hamper**.

I hang up clean clothes.

Next, I pick up my toys.

I put games in their boxes.

I put books on the shelf.

Stuffed animals go in
a basket.

Then I make my bed.

I **smooth** the sheets and blankets.

I put pillows on top.

Dusting and Vacuuming

Finally, I **dust** the shelves.

I **vacuum** the carpet.

That's how I cleaned my room.

How would you do it?

Activity

Write a Story

Pretend that you are responsible for cleaning up your room this afternoon. On a separate sheet of paper, write a story about the steps that you would take to do this job. Use at least three of the words shown on the opposite page to write your story.

Story Word List

first

next

then

last

before

after

finally

Fun Facts

- The easiest way to keep your room clean is to spend a few minutes picking up every day.

- Lots of kids share a room with a brother or a sister. Two people in one room means there is someone to help you clean!

- You can make cleaning your room fun! Try listening to music while you work. Or time yourself. Try to beat your record the next time you have to clean your room.

Glossary

dust – to clean by brushing away dirt

hamper – a basket with a cover that is often used to store dirty laundry

smooth – to make something flat and even with no lumps or wrinkles

vacuum – to clean using a machine that sucks up dirt

Index